Dear Big Gods

Dear Big Gods

Mona Arshi

First published 2019 by
Liverpool University Press
4 Cambridge Street
Liverpool
L69 7ZU

British Library Cataloguing-in-Publication data
A British Library CIP record is available

ISBN 978-1-78694-215-9 softback

Typeset by Carnegie Book Production, Lancaster
Printed and bound in Poland by Booksfactory.co.uk

for my jaan, Priya and Lily

Contents

Little Prayer

It's me
    again.
This time I'm a wren.

Last time I
    was the first
white sap.

Don't blow away
      the fruit flies
but visit my

pockets of blue-black
      pain. Little prayer
I am still here

hunkered down
      with the worm-casts
blind song

shrinking in
      my scratchy
after-feathers.

Narcissi

we begin in the gardens
more baffled by light than darkness
    sitting under the shade's chaperone
afraid to say
    that what we see inside our heads are
like tiny interruptions
    a gently blown leaf ... a bird resting on a wire
but aren't we all in that way
        reaching or
reaching for a troublesome child
    or an old fashioned malady
or surplus water
    feeding the flower?
maybe some of us are diverted to the
      mountain's fold
or others taking off our rings
      or others
being pulled into a pond
    our heads still full of the garden
full of narcissi ... or

a certain shape

clarified into

a purpling rose

our heads still full of narcissi

Everywhere

Mostly we are waiting for rain.
　　Sometimes we let
it fall gently
　　　　on our faces.
　　　　　　This is what a flower does.

Yesterday, I saw his eyes
　　in the eyes of a young man next
to the water-fountain.
　　　　　　We tell the children, we should not
　　　　　　look for him. He is everywhere.

He is everywhere.
　　We need not look in the black
sunflower seeds we take out for
　　　　　　the finches or between the blind
　　　　　　echoes of our prayers.

After rain, we lift up sheets of
　　canvas, nothing stirs,
like our own private church.
　　　　　We expect no answer –
　　　　　　though he must be there.

The Lilies

The lilies were sick.
I was new and wifely,
a first tiny garden and
my favourite flower right
by the back door.
They had been planted
in raised beds, all
self-conscious in
their outsized whiteness.
For weeks they seemed
fine, but then I noticed
a kind of injury, perforations
on the petals and a black
sticky gob –
            the fly's excrement.
I cleaned them up as best I could
but the blight returned.
In the dark with the kitchen lit
they must have peered in,
their occultish hurting faces
pressed against the glass.
They were hard to love back,
            these flowers.
I gave them nothing else,
spared them my gaze.
Those poor dazed heads.
I suppose I could have
pulled up their sick stems
or poisoned them from the bottle.
But I let them live on
            beauty-drained
in their altar beds.

Five-Year Update

I hope it's fine to contact you, to tell you that I still watch the gaps in the carriages
and listen out for 'the service has been disrupted' announcement, for some other poor sister's
new news. Five years ago the American women overheard my call just before Colchester.

They passed bottles of water and Granola bars to my seat; three women in their sixties
each with the same face powder. It's always the daughters, they say, it's always the same
graffiti over the bridge when you pass in the rain decades later though most insects are content

to fly through raindrops, so I've heard. As for the humming living, well, we are still
standing in the polluted shade whilst under us the choked-up sap retreats back into the soil
and there's us maggot-blind walking into rooms backwards, pacing. Or … diligently

pursuing our jumpy little grieflings, stalking those roly-poly sow bugs living-breeding
under the patio table. Yes, acceptance was something I believed in but all of a sudden
you are lying down and you are no longer tall but long (not to mention your arm that

mechanically pokes out of my dream like it's fishing). No-one profits from pitchy memory apart from Nepenthe's twisted therapist since you've gone to ashes now and we've turned the box into the water of the Thames near the dogwood, crying. Standing under a low roof

dirtying the window with our dirty hands, we've turned your trainers south facing into the indigo night, rest assured my bony-breath'd brother. Voices-voices-hence this update. Remember we counted yellow cars in our Fiat 128, but what's your perfect fuel now

O supersonic boy? Your Judge Dredd, crime-plagued futures gone to waste. I can't help but curse and what better use for breath you might say? I don't know about you but I've left part of myself in Inwood Park cozying up to a gold dog in the sunshine but only

after we'd rowed and you'd practised your katas on the so-green grass by the benches.

Which part of you was left there? The Egyptians, they have a name for it. I've been wearing my extravagant robes with the hems ruptured, the cord tied oh so loosely. How many breaths in later

I've got older but smaller, I've gone down one lump not two, I still don't swim and yes I still can't take a photograph. I see your face from time to time, especially on trains, where it flashes up in the gangway just before we slow right down and I reach for the door handle, alight and run to the barriers.

The Humble Insistence

of small things
you naked as a bird when
I touch your calloused wings

each branch knowing how not to touch
the shadow of a hand
disturbing too much

or the soundless waves of loss
under the bean tree
kneeling in moss

the childless rain, which comes and goes
the mewing angels
their shins exposed.

Tanka: I Loved You Best in Spring

I
The trees leak the sun
and the forest thinks in leaves.
But what you don't see:
the faintest lines on my face,
the allure of the unfinished.

II
Hand me your sorrows,
needy rivers you denied,
little boats of hope.
Birdsong aches its way to Spring,
somehow you pinch me awake.

III
Fast clouds laced with ink:
this is how the cold begins.
You're my accomplice
from a half-recovered dream;
a thin bleed on the brain.

IV
Undisturbed shadow,
silent as this flower's throat.
Sooner than you think
the gardens all surrender
to one sort of God I suppose.

V
What are you afraid of
when I kiss your shoulder?
Must you check my coat
pockets? Touch my hair again,
obedient in your hands.

Something

something scrambled out of me at least I thought
it was out of me it could have been into me
very fast very sly dirty breath'd assassin

spiders ants earthworms
I witnessed being dissected by my brothers
and crane flies I tried

but never managed to capture
whole such fey stupid wings and legs left drifting on walls
mostly I was a witness mostly

I've kept out of the way with
my hood zipped up to my chin
what is the surest thing we know?

that as we grow older we think less of
killing things and more of coming back
who knows where we acquire our knowledge

from our mothers aunts perhaps
they pass it on like a candle through
an ancient pockmarked door something parenthetic

like a clasp broken   useless as a rotten wick
a spider climbing the sublime coast
of your shoulders walking through those rooms again

a web breaking on the back of your hand

The Wasps

Suddenly they were on him. He was ten, the cricket game
abandoned, but already they drizzled over his limbs,
plunging into his ears, his eyes, trying to break
into his body. The children stood around him
screaming, stamping them out though he didn't howl
or stagger even, he was shaking his head moving
his arms – swiping in wide semi circles in some
horrible dance, just blind panic, adrenaline.
His hair was on fire. His dark boy-fringe lit by their frenzy
as these maniacal creatures, this colony, loaded with
pheromones ruffled around his neck. I was crying
held back by an aunt till someone brought the hose-pipe
and drowned them all. His lips were blue, red, swollen,
the ball still in the nest as the sober boy stood
dripping into the soil, into their soused bodies, spent.

The Switch

I found the Switch at precisely 6.05 pm. The Switch of all Switches; the primal Switch. I dug it out from beneath my arm with a pair of nail scissors and tested it on the insects on the window. I experimented through glass: street lamps flickered then went out, though when I pointed it up to Orion nothing happened. I switched off my boy when he cried (though I only did this once). I thought of all the good I could do with this Switch. I travelled to the Jumper's Cliff, and waited for the sight of live bodies, and switched them all off before they did it. On the train home I felt so tired and for the first time for a long time I slept, dreamlessly. When I woke I just knew the Switch had gone and I thought about lots of things : herded-up insects on the windowsill, those simple shapes on the cliff, indifferent to falling light, the glitter in the surf.

Fish

Oh but it was ugly. This fish, white-grey,
must have been old. It's ugliness was true
as the mountains we had just passed, the bait
that lured it, a pink-skirted baby octopus.
This old naked maiden fish had been
caught, its sad mouth trusted
the lurid rubber bait in the deep waters.
Near the engine in the box, dead fish lay
iced into submission but in the man's
hands, this one live unsquabbling fish.
Seconds later, its head resting on a crisp-
packet and in the syrupy afternoon light
it emptied out its loveliness – the streak of
reckless freckles glittering under an eye,
which reminds me now of a pregnancy mask.
Everyone but the children looked away
as the first mate took a spike to its brain.

Mirrors

after Federico Garcia Lorca's Mirror Suite

Symbol

Loose haired girl
a mirror in each hand
tilts her head
we are all somewhere beatific
aren't we?

The Giant Mirror

Oh cold collector of bruise
and flounce and
excess breath.
This woozy thirsty surface of want.

Reflection

[meanwhile a bowl
of clouds
thrashes blindly in
the alleyway ...]

Rays

In my photograph
of the mirror
blooms a flimsy-veined
soul clinging
to the surface like an octopus.

Replica

How we learn to break into mirrors.
My mother's old dressing table – smoky
winged mirrors-split shadows.

> [The other daughter sits sockless
> in the centre of four paperless
> walls like a compacted spirit.]

Earth

[all eleven years of me
tucked under a wallpaper branch-
ticking ...]

Capriccio

The way a mirror hunts for
the detail on
a redtail's foot trembling
on a branch.

Shinto

I pour myself in and
then out again
all my past lives
revolving.

Eyes

Outside my brother's rooms
there hangs a mirror
and thin hairless death
s l o p e s
on the bevelled edge.

Initium

like overstaked saplings
so patiently
we grow them
we lose them
she says
these overwrought
fibrous roots that
some girls retain

Berceuse for a Sleeping Mirror

In the olden days certain
cursed mirrors were walled up
never destroyed, much later
they added wilful brides
with small perfumed feet.

Air

The Sultan tried to coax it to talk but the mirror made bargains with no man. Its small eyes looked up at the Sultan defiantly. The Sultan asked his men to throw the mirror into the RIVER OF ANGUISH. Bird song ached through the forests where gallons of blood had been spilt. The river suffered as its river folk suffered, many inches of bone dust sat at the bottom. The villagers had left or had given up hope. The mirror finally looked up and asked to be put out of its misery.

Confusion

Nothing is as tragic
as a mirror-nothing
speaks quite so well of
bloodshot lonesomeness.

The Pool

A child climbing the footstool
to look –
holding the frame
to blow away the ants.

Like the first morning

I sit at the kitchen table where
the light is best, where the light is.
As mute as dawn, I blink her out,
examine her hands, ink-stained
and cold, her neck creaking like an
iron hinge cooling on a gate.
I search the patchpockets of
her dress, full of tiny perforated
shells and small yolk-coloured flowers
ruining the lining and I run my fingers along
her back and through her hair which flows
like lava across her pale collarbones.
When I flinch, she flinches, this
soft girl, this churning broken song.

*On a line from 'Morning Has Broken', a hymn
by Eleanor Farjeon.*

A Pear from the Afterlife

Our faces in the window float
        like balloons in the glass.
                In his deathness,

he never looked more alive.
                Sis, you gotta let go
                of this idea of definitive knowledge.

Don't look on it as a journey more
        like a resettling or dusting off or
                re-tuning of the radio.

There are elm trees here and these geckos
        slip surreptitiously under the door
                from my side to yours.

'Too bad you have to go back,' I say,
        and he sighs like an old man
                impatiently re-teaching a child.

'Before you go,' I say,
        'Will you bring me a pear from
                the afterlife or a ripe papaya or

even an accidental patch of clover,
        something that can live
                on my tiny balcony?'

'I was the slightest in the house'

Emily Dickinson

I was the slightest in the house
    & spoke in ampersand
quick & light & sparse & thin
    I seldom made a sound.

I held a rattle in my fist
    till I was nearly four
they dressed me up in skirts of wood
    mistook me for the floor.

One night my bird-blown heart awoke
    the forest called me in
its bubbling call; the moaning sap
    I stepped inside the hymn.

I bent my little tongue along
    the mouth parts of the tree
I was the slightest in the house
    arboreal & free.

Autumn Epistles

Once a thought, a September
thought, a girl's attendance at a table,
the crane flies
        fumbling in through
the louvres and her own striated
flight muscles flexing.

*

Later, a half-afraid boy
        I held his knee and
blew into the small tear of skin.

Even the forced flower
        withholds the indifferent
parts of herself.

*

And the bird that
rents out the branch
        that dutiful grip
as it listens
to the ant's attendance
along the same stem?

*

I am combing the grass
with my fingers.
Fuchsia burns out, leaves fall.
The leaf doesn't need
        to bend to fall into
the benevolent shapes of
an after-life.

Now I dream in
vine weevil
        and of gloveless hands
poking the exploding borders.
I count the birds
        my attendance at windows,
waiting rooms also
cracked fountains.

*

        I bend myself right back
to breath-filled knowing again,
the dormant mumble
        of well-water and the implied
lakes in our minds we
never hesitate to still.

'In Mexico the women are marrying trees.'

News Report, 2018

Last night I went all the way with a tree.
I headed to the forest, past the lake the
thicket of wild junipers, blossom still
young and mute, the insensible fungi
on the floor of the vast forest of leaves.
The others came, slipped in like silent
emissaries towards the dark colossal frame;
the waiting grooms. So many trees, we sighed,
so much loneliness. In the golden hour we
parted the bark then married them.
        If you press your ear to its body-
the oak, it doesn't sing, it rings, you follow
the sound deep inside – the speech is always
fettered to the root. We raved all night, our
impatient husbands still ringing out their oaths.

Ghazal: Darkness

Around the base of the trees amongst the broad oaks,
    I leave my daughters to ripen in the darkness.

Beneath the cunning soil's breath, sweet white snowdrops
    their strewn hearts are glowing in the darkness.

The soil thanks us; we roll up our cuffs,
    fill our pocket mouths defenceless in the darkness.

A gentle murmured refrain like old rain,
    snowflakes again we answer to the darkness.

I've seen those girls foraging for wild mushrooms,
    the rim around their retinas turning in the darkness.

We plant cloves, tiny armless gods into the loam,
    poke them deeper into the uncertainty of darkness.

My girls are distracted and starved of light,
    which is normal, which is essence of girl-darkness.

I slip outside and light a candle, cauterize a bud,
    Shabash I call to my girls, my praise in the darkness.

Now I know the Truth about Octopuses (and the lies we tell our children)

No mother could give more

Jim Cosgrove, Biologist

*How they fashion a pillow from their front tentacles
for their lovers*

The Police will come if you pull down your doll's knickers.

these adept navigators in the abyssal waters

We have nothing in common with the anxious foreigner.

... feetless, escapologists

That Helen went willingly.

these great rhapsodisers of the sea ...

Everything on your plate was tenderly coaxed into submission ...

how they love and live brightly

... yes even the lamb.

their engorged hearts pulsing (they have three)

Michael Jackson died because he ate too much butter.

standing vigil over their milky teardrop babies

The blurry defenseless bee is not worth fighting for.

forsaking food, forsaking comfort

That's hair on your body, not fur.

they live not long, unnourished

That sunlight smells of nothing.

their bodies fade …

Obedience. Obedience. Obedience.

their souls finding shelter
amongst the sea-grass

The Mango

In the age of reinvigorated nationalism
how does the mango fare?

News snippet 2016

Mango
sits on my desk
quietly, orangely (pinkish of belly)
discreetly carrying her
stone of shame
my undancing mango
not hurting anyone.

Delivery Room

Having you nearly killed me. The problem
with active veins is that I bruise like a peach.
My womb is shaking. I croak out some intensifiers
very   absolutely   utterly   totally   like
I am ready to push now. The doctor asks:
'Do you prefer the geometric or lyrical approach –
I am open to ideas?' 'Neither' I say. His paisley tie
swings like a pendulum over my belly.
When pain strikes it is lilac
against the colour of the walls, which are the colour
of Nice biscuits. In the milk of my mind I draw
a diagonal line and a perfect horizon –
'Have you ever ridden a penny farthing?'
'Is that important? Will I still get the morphine?'
'You are presenting very very posterior,' I hear the rest
of his team concur. One of them doses out the syringe,
the other one is crushing sugared almonds in her teeth.

Post Surgery, ICU, 3 a.m.

I am sitting in
the most dangerous seat
of the aeroplane with a perfumed heart
in my hands.

There is the tapping at my vein,
Come in, I say
and someone
attaches a blurry photograph

on the bedframe.
Several times
they tell me:

the babies are downstairs
all labelled and waiting.

Sabah is Missing

They had released all the girls but Sabah
was still missing.
Every other girl was accounted for but

Sabah was not home. The mother had
not stopped
praying for her,

the brothers never
took their eyes off the dusty road.
The rains had not neglected her,

the wheat seeds swelled and the sun
still fevered
in the cloudless sky without her.

The grandmother dreamt of
smelling the river of her
in her hair again.

The prophet's mouths slackened
against the beleaguered wind
that blew

the dust that still collected
in the kitchens around the tapered stems
of the old forever stools

and like this they waited.

Grief Holds a Cup of Tea

She balances a saucer on her lap
and confides — *I've had surgery on my lips,*
but is it too much, have I overdone it
this time?

*

The King died then the Queen died is a story
says the writer, the King died then the Queen
died of grief is a plot, but who will supervise
my departure she asks
who will pack my valise?

*

In the garden she prepares the soil by
sterilizing it with boiling water.
She repudiates moles with her
split-stance pose.
She spent 10,000 hours
perfecting this bendy technique.

*

She borrows a ladder and removes
the glazing pins from the
book-sized panes of the greenhouse
and one by one the ancient
glass panels lose their footing
from the grey putty.

*

She hands out stickers in the car park,
keeps off the grass
and gives me
a pair of royal blue slacks I
don't know what to do with.

*

Grief passes hard vowels
through a small frameless
window and snags
on the painted ledge.

The Village

When I pronounce silence I destroy it–
Wislawa Szymborska

Every morning the sun slides open and the people in the village are watchful. For some reason no one can quite remember all the pianos have been abandoned and instead the harmonium is the only instrument that's truly mastered. The Mayor has a professorial air though he has no education to speak of as there are no schools, universities or libraries. The waters (they say) have never been navigable and swimming is strictly prohibited.

The villagers occupy themselves with digging. Most families will own a set of spades forged by the country smiths, children are shown the local digging methods as soon as they are able to walk. The villagers pride themselves on inventing The Baron. It has an extra wide mouth and a side-wing, which can cut out the skin of the earth in one clean stroke. The people are adherents of the Old Faith; they recite passages of the ancient texts whilst they dig and on certain high holidays it is a sight to behold.

A part-blind woman who lives in the North is the oldest citizen. She is a witch (of sorts) but is a highly-cultured woman. If you visit, more often than not they will bring her to you. The village has its own coat of arms with a picture of a spade leaning on a simmal tree. The tree has lovely small red flowers and is considered holy, though it produces fruit, inedible even to the bats.

Sibling Discount

A phone number
slipped in his hand
outside a supermarket by a

woman wearing ripped jeans
and an REM t-shirt.
Then hand written messages:

I only flower when
you flower or
Zaungast (and no additional text).

Lucid. Punctual. Relatable.
Two weeks later they were
swapping match cards

whilst the rain rattled on pelting
the tin bowls on his balcony.
By January she had the front door key.

In February she'd removed her
spurs on the sofa stool
given him three cycles of song.

I called for him in Spring but
they said he was already gone.

The Department of Atrocities

You no longer wait in a powder-coated cell, you wait in comfort. Waiting is the new reposing in a vintage armchair facing the engraved portraits of the luminaries. The children are blindfolded, brought in standing on their own two feet, bodies turned, then slid onto their regulation-sized beds. Their rooms have been sprayed (in compliance with the executive orders) with flower essence issued by the DOA and the pillows plumped to the required height whilst the children sit marooned in quilted bed jackets. They are soothed by toys, hand-made, shipped in from the colonies; squadrons of shiny pubis bones from the finest turned ebony, walnut, sycamore. The men reinforce the two angled wooden beams (which cross the ceilings of this most ancient department) and arrange tighter fitting seals on the double-hung windows. Everyone waits for the allotted hour of the proclamation. At intervals the cartoon-clad nurses take the slow pulse of the children who rehearse each day with blunted pencils in their strangulated script.

The Sisters

In the dream, all the sisters I never had
hold a book of stars. I count them in and
count them out to the garden trampoline.
I never knew till now what they were for,
these dreams, translucent skins.
In the wake, I take it all in through the vibrations –
I want the bones to be identified.
           But in the dream
I am running, hoping I might reach them and
throw a blanket around their shoulders.

Let the Parts of the Flower Speak

pedicel

You think you have illumed me
because you have translated me?
Please read me variantly with
a green fevered mind.

ovary

There's nothing sharp in
this house. All my terrors
my crowded out babies, half/half-
trembling little faces of gold.
I have no other vision than this.

filament

I have certain tendencies and these
tendencies may conflict with your
tendencies most certainly.

petal/*izaat*/respect

What would a faithful
rendering have demanded?
Petal etiquette;
how does one bear it?
bharish/bimaree.
This is my dharma
turning yellow after
initial growth.

stamen

The curse: almost certainly mis-
pronounced by a man.
Draw me faithfully: bitch, stable-witch,
what does my ambiguity permit?

style

I am not observant,
Why are you bringing
God into this?
And this my love
is going nowhere.

sepal

My little bastard verses
tiny polyglot faces
how light you are
how virtually weightless.

anther

Speak into me with your
mouth close to my
humming surface
beyond flower memory
piercing
leaf and loam
past rootlets
through the
aortic arch
glinting hearts of the
rosy-tipped worm.

Draupadi's Hair

After the disrobing of Draupadi in the Kaurava's Palace
(*The Mahabharata*)

It was like the first time I closed my eyes
properly, unbidden I opened them again
when I entered the walls of the Old City.
Sorrow heavy, I could barely walk
through the chest high reeds, the women
flinching when they saw my unbound hair.

The smell of the Palace was still in my hair.
They led me to their homes, their eyes
never left me. I was saved by these women.
They found me a place to lie and again
I suffered, fevered for days and sleepwalked
alone around the skein of the Old City.

You may have heard tales of the Old City?
Its breath so toxic I hid in the long hairs
of the *bohr* tree. Girls pitied me, walked
away shaking their heads, averting their eyes.
I swear I'll never crave anything again.
How to explain to innocents and women?

Pinch out my tears I say to the women:
my anger is a yellow lake, the starved city
can't contain it, when shall I begin again?
Five suns, five brothers, never reach my hair.
The tips of the mountains blind the eyes
of the sky and I need to rehearse and walk.

Long fingers of grief hold me as I walk
around my feathered shadow. The women's

stories flow fast and true, within their eyes
are tiny blessings. I will leave this city,
when the new rain comes and rinses my hair,
soaking the forever sloping stone again.

Look, I've begun to turn porous again.
Mothers tell us to dream corpses that walk
through rice-pale faces and as for my hair,
never speak of it to another woman.
I am a Queen with a song for this city
which jangles under the weight of its eyes.

The women of this city help me wear
my delicate risk of wings again,
one stops to lift the hair from my eyes.

Draupadi's Terror

Unguarded roof and my elbow bent in the water.
Maybe you hear a mumble from the shadows and
you call out? Or you recognize the smell perhaps
of lychees gently rotting in their crates? Our hands
still tremble as if from a recent dream and we button
our cardigans against it. They say they found hyena bones
in the cup-bearers' cave but hurry past those ghosts
that bloom, don't look beneath your feet.
I will tell you everything if you listen or leave your
mouth open to let the rain in, the eyelid closing
like a blessing, a blister resurfacing or the sudden
stain of lilac on your baby son's tunic. Wipe your lips
with this, narrow your eyes to squint, as the clouds
meet the trail again like a shadow that spills over and over.

Draupadi's Prophecy

I diluted it having captured it under a glass
    paperweight. I tried stroking, peeling and
screwing it. At some juncture I thought I might

scorch it with a pair of fire-tongs. There was
    nothing to be done but still I warmed alms
with betel juice, horse spit and ate it.

I moved to morphine after Zolpidem and
    small yellows. I tested every variety of nasal spray
and capsicum on my tongue. I used warm

olive oil dropped in real slow into each ear canal.
    There were Zoroastrians, pundits and preachers,
ayruvedics, heptologists and soothsayers.

During the days I squatted inside cool-
    lipped basins, I hid from it among the fissures
in the dark compounds at night.

Gloaming

They say this house was built on an orchard
and there are freckling pears lying on the grass
their skin barely contains their flesh.

I lost a girl once, in some woods I thought
I knew like the back of my hand,
both of us on bikes, her small head

sealed in the white helmet
bobbing through the branches
as she descended into the hush.

Like so many, I've squandered hours
waiting for the miracle in a temple
where a statue was crying.

I've been distracted by my own neat row
of mirrors before taking my seat
on crowded trains, our knees not touching.

My father asks for his bread softened in milk
then gags on cashews on his morning walk.
My mother licks stamps before the full

fall of dark – *gloaming* they call it in Scots.
Now my little mother is
entering/leaving through a narrow lintel

the rain spitting in her hair-parting
as I unfold and refold the umbrellas.
The thick soup of our childhood,

peat and rain we'd stir with sticks,
and then a girl looking up and asking
where are you from, what country are we in?

Odysseus

Mean Odysseus.
Like that time you returned
with a gull caught in your hair and
your sandals chafing,
how you outcried me.
Odysseus and your trinkets, your
pockets clacking with castanets.
God, how I scraped up
my misery and held it
up to the mirror,
a double sacrifice, divided
and simplified, and how
you smiled into my face
yellow-teethed from years
of *paan* eating!

My Third Eye

On the seventh day when my third eye still hadn't opened,
   I decided to return to Shree Gopal Ji Shree Rastri,
      at the palm leaf library. Everyone else's eyes had opened

      apart from mine. Sebastian's eyes had opened, Anjuna's eyes,
   even Sky's eyes had flowered and opened right up. They were
all in the kitchen breakfasting on the ripe papaya, the women

and the men too wearing frangipani in their hair and they
   sat content, filtered and glowing in the sunlight, such is the
      simple state of grace that visits you after full enlightenment.

      More perplexed than annoyed, I engaged a tuk tuk driver,
   a willowy man who swooned like a coconut tree when he bent
to lift my bags and whose eye had opened many summers ago.

We went on our way in the midday heat and a buffalo stepped
   onto our path (whose young monsoon eyes had already opened).
      When we arrived I sought out the miniature man with the

      squirrel paint brushes who squatted barefoot next to the carved
   sheesham library doors, *Am I not as worthy as the buffalo, the ferryman,*
the cook and the Dalit? I asked, looking into his old, pinprick eyes.

The holy man smiled and placed his blessing hand on my head
   and with that my eyes suddenly watered, widened and
      he sent me on my way as I was forever open open open.

Pomegranate

This is praiseworthy,
this fatigued ball
my whole life through I've asked-

if I praise enough;
when does wisdom come, little beads,
little teeth, if not from the

light praising of lit things?
Have I not praised enough?
You bled into my pocket once,

little one, do you remember,
unused to being cloaked,
a minor dishonour, but you

bled out brightly in the sunshine.
Then my daughter was born
with a god-given egg nestled

by her shoulder
which lay there a while
auditioning softly on her chest.

By the month's end it was
tapping and weeping.
So I will praise you openly now

By the cooling flowers where
I set aside my notebook and
the pencil I let drop.

Poem

Someone somewhere is reading
the same poem as me.
The ivy is suffocating the holly tree and

a child is learning to unlisp.
A dog's forepaws rest
on his old master's frame

and someone is reading
the same poem as me.
The phone sits on the raspberry doily.

The girls get up and brush their
knees, push their naked feet
back into their shoes and the Eurasian tree sparrow

moves its cryptic mouth towards a beetle.
Somewhere, a boy is trespassing on a train line
under a queasy sunset and

by a hospital bed a son kisses
the damp strangeness of his
father's palm, a tear catching in his beard.

A daughter is salting the aubergines.
Her sister spins a tiny planet in a classroom
far, far, from here.

Because you left no note

i've invented one instead
you can ruin yourselves with words
the pulse taps out ampersands
ask anyone who's experienced birth pangs or
    reverse birth pangs

i find your *inter alia* in the rubbish bin with
the secret ingredient for gunpowder
i skin an *etcetera* and smoke it
    return the shiver to the air

When Your Brother Steps into your Piccadilly, West Bound Train Carriage

You do not stare or question him about the after-life
those mythical pears, the balconies and the
     how-the-fuck-could-you?
You could give up your seat, lean forward to touch the hem of
his denim shirt, pull gently on his head-phone wires, say
I am sorry, I'm so sorry.

Dear Big Gods

all you have to do
is show yourself
in case you hear us
we are so small
and fenceless in the shade
throw us a hook
when you can
touch the scribbled
child in the inferno
all you have to do
is show yourself a little
pin your dark
olive green parts
against the boulder

Acknowledgments

I am once again indebted to my editor, Deryn Rees-Jones, for her belief in the book and careful reading and editorial support.

Thanks are due to the editors of the following publications in which some of these poems or versions of them first appeared: POETRY; Poetry Review, The Guillemot Press, Wild Court Magazine, The White Review, The Moth, Oxford Review, The Well Review, The Scores, Modern Poetry in Translation and The Dizziness of Freedom (Bad Betty Press). 'Ghazal: Darkness' was first broadcast on BBC Radio 4, Book of the Week: Odysseus, The Patron Saint of Foreigners?

I am deeply indebted to Mimi Khalvati for teaching me so much about poem making. I am returning the blessing here – 'The Humble Insistence' is dedicated to her.